Breezier, Cheesier, Newest, and Bluest

What Are Comparatives and Superlatives?

To my friends at Hainerberg Elementary School in
Wiesbaden, Germany

—B.P.C.

Comparatives:
Forms of describing
words that compare
two things

Superlatives:
Forms of describing
words that compare
three or more things

Breezier, Cheesier, Newest, and Bluest

What Are Comparatives and Superlatives?

by Brian P. Cleary

illustrations by Brian Gable

M̲ MILLBROOK PRESS / MINNEAPOLIS

comparatives

all help describe things.
Most end in e-r,

like hotter day
and longer way
and faster, sleeker car.

See how they compare two things,
like long when paired with longer?

They help distinguish by degree,
like strong
compared with stronger.

7

cooler, crueler,

louder, prouder,

hairier, and scarier—

these are all comparatives,
like mellower and merrier.

Try taking a describing word, like bright.

Now add e-r.

You've made it a comparative to name the *brighter* star!

But sometimes, you don't add e-r. Instead, you reach for "more,"

as in more tired, **ZZZ**

more beautiful,

and more impressive store.

other times, comparatives,
like those I've listed here,

seem to have no type of rule
to which they all adhere.

Superlatives compare as well
but speak of an extreme—

the tallest girl, the longest curl,
the highest balance beam.

"Tall" is a describing word,
and **taller** is comparative.

Tallest is **Superlative.**
You following my narrative?

Most times, a superlative will end in e-s-t:

the meanest dog,

the greenest frog,

the fanciest TV.

It's one up from comparative, like newest topping newer,

BEST

BETTER

GOOD

smartest up from smarter,

and bluest over bluer.

Superlatives are breeziest

and chattiest

and cheesiest,

funniest and sunniest

and quietest and queasiest.

But e-s-t is not the end for some superlatives.

Most modern and most fun
are two examples I can give.

These words can be quite difficult,
but study them with zest

So What are comparatives and Superlatives? Do you know?

How to Form Comparatives and Superlatives

Usually, add -er or -est to the end of the adjective (describing word).

| tall | taller | tallest |
| long | longer | longest |

If a one-syllable adjective ends in an e, simply add -r or -st.

| blue | bluer | bluest |
| large | larger | largest |

If a one-syllable adjective ends in a consonant with a vowel right before it, double the consonant before adding -er or -est.

| big | bigger | biggest |
| thin | thinner | thinnest |

If an adjective ends in y, change the -y to -i and add -er or -est.

| happy | happier | happiest |
| lucky | luckier | luckiest |

With many other two-syllable adjectives, use "more" or "most."

| pleasant | more pleasant | most pleasant |
| thoughtful | more thoughtful | most thoughtful |

Other adjectives don't follow any pattern.

far	farther	farthest
bad	worse	worst
many	more	most

Find activities, games, and more at
www.brianpcleary.com

ABOUT THE AUTHOR & THE ILLUSTRATOR

BRIAN P. CLEARY is the author of the best-selling Words Are CATegorical® series as well as the Math Is CATegorical®, Food Is CATegorical™, Animal Groups Are CATegorical™, Adventures in Memory™, and Sounds Like Reading® series. He has also written *Do You Know Dewey? Exploring the Dewey Decimal System*, *Six Sheep Sip Thick Shakes: And Other Tricky Tongue Twisters*, and several other books. Mr. Cleary lives in Cleveland, Ohio.

BRIAN GABLE is the illustrator of many Words Are CATegorical® books and the Math Is CATegorical® series. Mr. Gable also works as a political cartoonist for the *Globe and Mail* newspaper in Toronto, Canada.

Millbrook Press
A division of Lerner Publishing Group, Inc.
241 First Avenue North
Minneapolis, MN 55401 USA

For reading levels and more information, look up this title at www.lernerbooks.com.

Main body text set in RandumTEMP 35/48.
Typeface provided by House Industries.

Library of Congress Cataloging-in-Publication Data

Cleary, Brian P., 1959—
    Breezier, cheesier, newest, and bluest : what are comparatives and superlatives? / by Brian P. Cleary ; illustrations by Brian Gable.
        p.   cm. — (Words are CATegorical)
    ISBN 978—0—7613—5362—1 (lib. bdg. : alk. paper)
    ISBN 978—1—4677—1053—4 (eBook)
    1. Grammar, comparative and general—Adjective—Juvenile literature. 2. Comparison (Grammar)—Juvenile literature. I. Gable, Brian, 1949—, ill. II. Title.
P273.C54 2013
428.1—dc23   2012019105

Manufactured in the United States of America
2 — DP — 9/1/14